CHARLES FAUDREE

COUNTRY FRENCH LEGACY

CHARLES FAUDREE
COUNTRY FRENCH LEGACY

Photographed and Written by
JENIFER JORDAN

GIBBS SMITH
TO ENRICH AND INSPIRE HUMANKIND

First Edition

19 18 17 16 15   5 4 3 2 1

Published by

Gibbs Smith

P.O. Box 667

Layton, Utah 84041

1.800.835.4993 orders

www.gibbs-smith.com

Designed by Sheryl Dickert and Renee Bond

Printed and bound in China

Gibbs Smith books are printed on either recycled, 100% post-consumer waste, FSC-certified papers or on paper produced from sustainable PEFC-certified forest/controlled wood source. Learn more at www.pefc.org.

Library of Congress Cataloging-in-Publication Data

Jordan, Jenifer.
 Charles Faudree country French legacy / Photographed and written by Jenifer Jordan. — First Edition.
 pages cm
 ISBN 978-1-4236-3854-4
1. Faudree, Charles—Themes, motives. 2. Interior decoration--United States. 3. Decoration and ornament, Rustic—France—Influence. I. Title.
 NK2004.3.F38J67 2015
 747.092—dc23
 2014034364

In celebration of Charles Faudree:
his beautiful heart, his love and friendship
to many, his distinctive design talent,
and his love of all things Country French.

CONTENTS

FOREWORD BY BILL CARPENTER | 9

PREFACE BY JENIFER JORDAN | 11

INTRODUCTION | 15

ENTRIES & HALLWAYS | 17

LIVING ROOMS | 37

CLUBROOMS & LIBRARIES | 68

DINING ROOMS | 97

KITCHENS | 117

BEDROOMS | 139

BATHROOMS, CLOSETS & DRESSING ROOMS | 177

OUTDOOR SPACES | 197

ACKNOWLEDGMENTS | 208

FOREWORD
BY BILL CARPENTER

Where does one begin in talking about a man like Charles Faudree? He held a certain type of magic, like the Pied Piper, that caused people to follow his lead. In the process "his followers" fell in love with his energy, enthusiasm, talent, humor and zest for life! He was known as the master of Country French style. This was truly a gift—coming from Muskogee, Oklahoma, Charles's hometown—having that innate style and vision of his signature look. His look evolved and changed throughout the years. It was never trendy and was always timeless. This book shows his design legacy, which is oh, so Charles.

Jenifer Jordan has photographed for Charles for more than twenty-seven years, beginning with regional field editor Nancy Ingram and *Traditional Home* magazine. This book includes the broad scope of Charles's career, including Jenifer's images of his earlier works as well as his last completed projects. She shows how his look has withstood the test of time and yet has evolved and changed. Charles's work is simply amazing.

Then there is Charles the person. What a great brother, partner, friend, teacher and clown. He was a devoted partner to me, a doting brother to Francie, and a great friend to many. Some remarked at his memorial service that he had 300 best friends. He never met a stranger and always had time to listen. He was gracious, humble, and will be missed by many. Charles remarked many times that he had one more book in him. I am sorry he was not able to see it, but I hope you all will enjoy this look at his Country French design legacy.

Facing: Lila and Ruby nap on a French chair covered in "Dauphine/Teal" from the Charles Faudree Collection for Stroheim.

Above: In a beautiful outdoor Jamaican breezeway, a pair of 19th-century French iron chairs flanks a 1940s French bronze table with a faux bronze marble top.

PREFACE

BY JENIFER JORDAN

I have had the privilege of photographing five of Charles Faudree's Country French design books; it is with love and honor that I present his sixth book, *Charles Faudree Country French Legacy*.

I met Charles in 1987 when I was hired to photograph his home for a Christmas issue for *Traditional Home* magazine with Nancy Ingram, regional field editor. I remember it vividly. It was a hot, humid October day in Oklahoma when I walked into the most beautiful, opulent Christmas setting I had ever seen. It was a memorable surprise, stunning! There were bows, ornaments, wreaths, decorated trees and flowers making it a Christmas wonderland like only Charles could do—with style.

Fast forward to 2002 and many fun photography shoots of his work with Charles and Nancy for national interior design magazines and books. The three of us thought we should do our own design book together. I crudely prepared a book prototype; I literally cut and pasted images and faux text onto pages into a small book. The one prototype acquired some tattered pages and a few rejections before we found Gibbs Smith publisher. We completed what we set out to do, our first design book, *Charles Faudree's French Country Signature*. The book was well received and Charles created quite the following across the country. Over the next few years we added four more volumes to our library, including *Charles Faudree's Country French Living, Charles Faudree Interiors, Charles Faudree Details* and *Charles Faudree Home*.

Charles's style was unique and very distinctive. In the twenty-seven years of photographing with this incredible talent, I was always amazed and inspired when I walked into one of the beautiful homes he designed. As the photographer, I walked in, of course, when the rooms were photo-ready; every pillow was, as Charles would say, "poofed"; fresh flowers were in place; every book and design element was artistically placed and fires were roaring in the fireplaces. It was Charles's beautiful vision, but it was my joyous task to photograph and document every detail and record his Country French legacy. As an interior photographer, I see in two-dimensional vignettes and could visually see images for the printed page. There was eye candy everywhere I looked. I could shoot

Facing: A painted Swedish secretary is the pivotal piece in a light-filled breakfast room.

"We miss that wonderful, adorable, man with impeccable taste and the twinkle in his eye. He will always be a part of our lives and we remember him with fondness and treasured memories." –LINDA JAMES

Posing for one of our book photographs, I could hardly contain my laughter from one of Charles's jokes. He was the funniest man I ever met!

for days in one location and had a hard time editing the images. In the five books I did with Charles—now six—I hope my photographs of his work illustrated and portrayed his undeniable talent and his aesthetic.

I looked forward to every one of our photo shoots, in anticipation of not only seeing Charles's magical talent but of spending time and laughing with my dear friend. I can honestly say that Charles was the funniest person I have ever known. It was not all business all the time! He would make me laugh so hard that sometimes I could not catch my breath. His many jokes included prank calls. I am sure if you have been the recipient of these calls you are laughing right now. Mine was a phone call from an old woman saying she was my neighbor down the street. "Do you have two yellow lab dogs? They just ran past my house!" Startled, I dropped the phone, but there were Sister and Sadie sitting right beside me. He got me. I picked up the phone and Charles was laughing and laughing.

Once I was setting up a shot and had to move a few things to correct tangencies through the camera. I got closer and there was a red puddle of a spilled bottle of bright red fingernail polish on this very expensive Louis XVII fine antique commode! I quickly grabbed it thinking, "Oh, no!" Charles was laughing at me picking up his plastic fingernail polish joke in a panic.

The biggest gotcha was in Spain, where we were shooting an incredible villa. The home had one of those faux life-size butlers. We had been shooting for three days and Charles was busy having the butler "pop up" for a startle and a laugh all over the villa, scaring everyone. The last night of the shoot, I thought I was free from the joke. We had to get up by 4 a.m. for an early flight. I wearily walked into the shower—and screamed!

Six days before his passing, Charles and I reminisced about fun times, and he even spoke of us doing another book when he was feeling better. I believe Charles wanted his friends, family and readers to see the last projects he was working on. I hope this book would have fulfilled that desire.

"Au revoir cher ami." Good-bye, dear friend.

—Jenifer

INTRODUCTION

Facing: One of Charles's favorite French chairs in one of his favorite fabrics, "Beauclaire," from the Charles Faudree Collection for Vervain.

"In the language of interior design, I would like to think I have helped elevate French Country to a fine art. It is an excessive, exuberant style that fosters my favorite design principle—too much is never enough. With my love for mixing past and present, old and new, I like to create inviting rooms that express a casual, comfortable feeling. I am often guided by my belief that there are no rules about where you can use things. That's why French Country design has a pleasing, fluid quality and an appeal that is timeless." —Charles Faudree, from *French Country Signature*

As elegantly stated in *Charles Faudree's French Country Signature*, Charles achieved an international reputation for creating settings that have all the elegant accoutrements of a French Country estate. It was Charles's union of the rustic with the refined that created his distinctive style of casual, understated elegance.

Charles was often asked to define his style, to elaborate on the secret of French Country signature. He would respond, "Oh, it's all in the mix, not the match. Hopefully, that mix is always artful, eclectic and inspiring. I believe there is an art to arranging and accessorizing. I try to create what is pleasing to look at, what is appropriate and in balance for the room."

In this book, *Charles Faudree: Country French Legacy*, there are many examples of how Charles's design began with a pivotal item that would dictate the style and design for the whole room. He brought order and balance with symmetrical groupings, while always creating a room that reflected the personalities and lives of those that lived there. Charles expressed his passion for layering by mixing old and new objects from different centuries and countries, and mixing fabric textures and prints, giving each room soul.

In the following pages, experience Charles Faudree's legacy and his wonderful journey through the design process. There is new photography of his last projects as well as selected images from his five previous books.

I would never claim to be an authority on Country French design, but Charles Faudree certainly was. This book draws upon excerpts of his own words from his previous books, along with thoughts from his family, friends and clients.

As Charles would sign his books, "Enjoy, with fond wishes, *merci beaucoup!*"

Entries &
HALLWAYS

The first impression of a home often begins at the front door . . . It is important to also decorate a front porch, a porte cochere or even a back entry to set the tone for the rest of the home and to greet guests . . . If the exterior of a house entices, the interior—especially the entryway—must enthrall. I believe that first impressions are lasting, so it is important to make entries welcoming and inviting. I like entries that provide a clue or glimpse of what the rest of the house will look like." —Charles Faudree

A strong impression was also part of each homeowner's experience at their first meeting with Charles. Patricia Massey relates that she called Charles to see if he would help her with her home in Texas. Charles replied, "Let's meet to see if we like each other."

"I knew it was the beginning of a beautiful friendship," Patricia said. At first meetings, Charles also shared some of his design philosophy. One thing he always said was, "'No' is a complete sentence." He accepted a client's right to say no.

"Well, sometimes," says Gayle Eby, "The last time I said 'no' was at the Paris flea market two years ago. He had fallen in love with an 18th-century French column, absolutely fallen in love with it! Walked around it, left the shop, came back in, walked around it again, asked if I knew anybody who might need it—'No'—went to lunch, went back to the shop, walked around it again; he asked, 'Don't you need this?' 'NO!' He bought a little picture frame and then, giving one last look at the column, stated, 'You need this in your entry.' 'Yes!' That entry is now referred to by my family as the 'petite Place de la Concord.' Oh, how I loved my time with Charles!"

Charles said hallways are needed architecturally, to connect different parts of the home or to join a new addition to the main house. He also said a hallway is more than a bypass. It can be functional as well as beautiful, offering temporary resting areas with seating. It also can be another place to add a homeowner's beautiful collection of plates around a mirror or over an antique commode.

Facing: An antique painting of a military man stands watch as guests enter Charles and Bill's back entry, which displays a few of his favorite French treasures. Greeting guests was not the only purpose of this multi-functional back entry. Lilu and Ruby always knew where their treats were.

Above: A grouping of Jimmy Steinmeyer's original interior renderings lines the stairway.

"*After our first meeting I thought there could be no other way to possibly build our home without him. We met with him for a year and a half for at least an hour a week. My husband wouldn't miss a meeting and would always ask, 'When do we see Charles this week?'*" –LINDA JAMES

Facing: The old stone floor and logs with chinking make a wonderful backdrop for the entry in the Jameses' magnificent log home. A collection of antique botanicals flanks an antique cabinet, while a cozy daybed covered in "Oak & Acorn/Green" from the Charles Faudree Collection for Vervain greets guests.

Left: The hallway connecting the new clubroom to the dining room offers a cozy seating area.

"My husband once found a treasure trove of tapestry paintings, which Charles had framed for us. On his next trip to our home, he hung two of them over the sofa in our entry. He hung the extra tapestry on the landing to our master bedroom. I was not too sure about it and suggested it may be one too many tapestry paintings. He told me to wait, he had a plan. The next time he visited our home, he surprised us by completing the landing to our master with a stunning Dennis & Leen table, a pair of rock crystal lamps, and a barometer from his most recent trip to France. To perfection, he placed just one of our tortoiseshell boxes on the table. 'Now that's a picture,' he remarked on our landing before he left for Tulsa." —GINNY WEBB

Facing: The light-filled entry in the Webb home is the perfect spot for their grand piano and wonderful collection of tapestry prints.

Below: Charles paired the stunning oversized painted trumeau mirror with the antique commode and a pair of small French side chairs.

"Charles combined many of the treasures from our travels to fill our home with a warmth and beauty that he is known for. The fabrics are from the Charles Faudree line that he was so proud of. Many of our 'ditzying' items (as he called them) are from local Cashiers stores. I was able to spend almost every day with Charles in Cashiers that summer and will always treasure it."

—ROSEMARY HARRIS

Facing: Laura and Reeder Ratliff's spacious entry showcases Charles's classic use of symmetry, with a pair of brackets and a pair of French chairs flanking an antique trumeau mirror and commode.

In Dru Hammer's entry is a faux butler. "When the butler arrived to the new home we had just finished, he came in a pine box with straw. When the box was pried open, Charles let out a scream and thought a dead relative had been sent to us," Dru laughs.

A few inviting entries, from grand and formal to a back-door entry of a weekend cabin.

Left: The 19th-century blackamoor on the Louis XV commode greeted many of Charles's guests throughout the years.

Right: A faux butler and a magnificent Donald Sultan painting titled Twelve Butterflies *greet guests as they enter the home.*

"My entry is an expression of my love of all things French, especially Country French antiques."

—CHARLES FAUDREE

Facing: Coral accent pillows on a French Directoire-style settee along with a 19th-century brass Dutch chandelier bring delight and drama to the entry of a Jamaican villa.

"I decided not to paint the wood in the entry of our house, and Charles said 'Ohhhhh, I would have painted my mother if she would have stood still long enough!' Charles loved paint."

—KELLY GANNER

Traditional, Transitional and Modern: here are six examples showing Charles's talent in helping homeowners welcome their guests with style.

Facing left: Charles's motto "It's not the match but the mix" is exquisitely illustrated with a wonderful lantern overhanging a pair of antique candelabras and a modern blue bowl.

Antique clocks are one hallmark of a Charles-designed hallway. He frequently positioned a tall clock at the end to give definition and focus.

*Facing: A Directoire trumeau mirror centers the setting on a landing.
A collection of hand-colored bird engravings and a pair of French-style
side chairs fill out the space.*

Facing: Light streams into this glorious entry, elegantly furnished in French antiques, including a Régence fruitwood commode and a pair of Régence fauteuil oreilles, wing chairs.

Living
ROOMS

The rich fullness of furnishings and fabrics and an artful use of symmetry characterize many of the living rooms I design. Living rooms are overflowing but never cluttered or overpowering, even in the smallest of spaces. Part of the charm of a living room is a skillful blend of rustic and refined antiques and furnishings, with fabrics, colors, collections and accessories that create a beautiful, cohesive room. Color is the key that blends this rich mix of patterns—toile, paisley, stripes, plaids, florals—into a visually appealing display."
—Charles Faudree

Delineating rooms into separate conversation areas with symmetrical groupings was a hallmark of Faudree design. In large living rooms, if space allowed, he would create the main grouping underneath a central chandelier with a sofa and pairs of chairs.

The use of pairs creates an elegant living space, whatever the style. Pairs of sofas and chairs upholstered in neutral, complementary fabrics create a stylish palette for a room. Pairs of ottomans provide a pleasing departure from the identical matching chairs scheme.

Every Faudree design project began with a pivotal piece; each room often began with a pivotal fabric, a dominant color, or one magnificent antique, usually of French or English ancestry.

"The pivotal piece could also be a painting, a grand mirror, carved French urns, an antique mantel, or an antique trumeau. Just one distinctive piece of furniture, such as a towering armoire, an unusual commode, or a great accessory like a grand mirror or painting, will make the rest of the room seem more important," Charles said.

His signature design always included comfort. "Comfortable seating should never be a victim of great style," he said. "Even in the most elegant of rooms, the furnishings should be comfortable and incorporate luxurious pillows."

Facing: In Charles and Bill's living room the neutral backdrop showcases the pivotal fabric, "Le Marchand D'Etoffes/Craie" by Pierre Frey, on the pillows and on a wonderful mix of French chairs.

Facing: Charles was the master of the mix even in his own living room, mixing wonderful antiques, modern art and a modern Lucite coffee table.

"Comfortable seating should never be a victim of great style."
—CHARLES FAUDREE

"Elegant" begins to describe the Webbs' living room. The neutral subtle wall finish and sisal rug create a lovely backdrop for the room with comfortable furnishings.

"Pivotal fabrics! A room cannot proceed without a pivotal fabric."

—JULIE WELCH CUSHING CHARLES

A mix of fabrics in grays, blue-grays, taupes and a little mint is stunning in the McCubbins' living room.

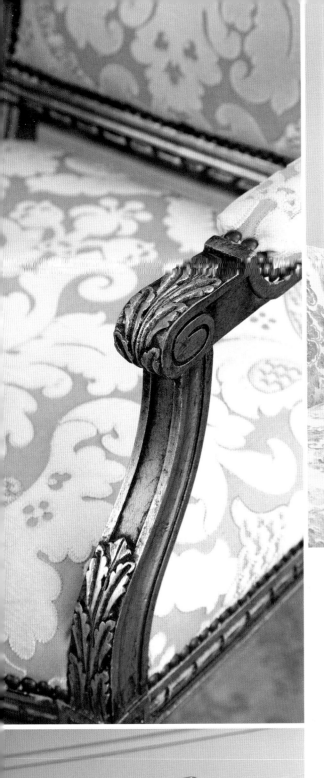

"In my new living room, I wanted a cleaner look than I had before. Charles mixed monochromatic neutral fabrics on my sofa and pairs of chairs with a few country French pieces for symmetry and balance." –GAYLE ALLEN

Modern art and a pair of iron Dennis & Leen wrought-iron wall sconces elegantly hang above the mantel in the Ratliffs' light and bright living room with wonderful architectural beams.

Along with the furnishings, Charles's Country French design concepts extended to the smallest details. "Details may seem like a small subject, but these finishing accessories are by far the most important part of decorating. People's lives are expressed by little details. They give the room its soul," he said.

Left: "Florentine Damask" by Beaumont & Fletcher is the pivotal fabric covering the sofa and miniature bergère as well as draping the windows. A wonderful bow-front Louis XV commode from southwestern France is the perfect place to showcase a pair of antique dog lamps with custom shades.

"I always remembered Charles saying 'Deceit by disguise!' Less expensive fabric for drapes—fabulous fringe and trims!"

—ANN OSBORNE

"We remember one fabric in particular that we had tossed to the side. A few minutes later, he reappeared with yards of the flowing fabric draped around him, dancing smoothly across the room. How could you resist?"

—KATHY KUCHARSKI

"Too often people go to a lot of trouble to create a perfect room and stop just before they've made it truly theirs." —CHARLES FAUDREE

"Charles was very talented and adaptable to his clients' needs. He was delighted beyond words that he could share his signature look, which was limitless and, of course, timeless." —GAYLE ALLEN

"There was nothing like seeing the spark in his eyes and feeling the electricity in the room when the perfect combination of fabrics was chosen!" —REBECCA McCUBBIN

"On another expedition we came upon a shop that was all things pewter. We ended up with a pile of pewter treasure on the floor. Charles asked, 'So, Cassie, how long have you been collecting pewter?' I was dumbfounded. 'All your life!' he supplied." —CASSIE SHIRES

"Once Charles and I were hanging a painting on a brick wall in the client's kitchen. The client was with us. Charles started hammering the nail, but the nail didn't go into the brick; instead it flew across the room and hit the client in the head." —GEORGE FADAOL

"Charles would look at the final design impact, not necessarily the amount of money spent. For example, for my mantel I bought a mirror at an estate sale for less than fifty dollars. Charles had the mirror painted with an incredible finish to make it look like an expensive antique. He then added a pair of expensive iron bouquets, a few glass obelisks and a candle to complete the beautiful impact over the mantel." –GAYLE ALLEN

Previous overleaf: An antique horse oil painting proudly sits on the mantel of the fabulous stacked stoned fireplace in Rosemary Harris and Tracy Spears' Cashiers living room.

Above: Charles captured the essence of pure comfort and luxury. Who couldn't relax or enjoy a roaring fire in the Jameses' cabin living room in blues, tans and browns in this Cashiers log cabin living room? Lily and Parker, my adorable Cavalier rescues, made themselves right at home.

"Sitting at the long table in the back room of his shop, surrounded by floor-to-ceiling shelving laden with fabrics, Diet Coke on ice, we played. We started with the large living area. . . . I think we used 11 different fabrics . . . some of them more than once in that room, beginning with the focus fabric, a stylized floral. Charles laid out the game pieces: big checks, stripes, solids, animal print and toile. I could begin to imagine his vision. The palette was in a brown and sage green colorway, like the colors of the lake and trees, a perfect mix." –CASSIE SHIRES

"And then there was Paris! Flea market mania from dawn to dusk. Charles was known to all in the stalls and shops. We arrived at the market on a Wednesday afternoon in order to get super-duper deals. In three hours time, I had bought one armoire, two secretaries, and nineteen chairs! All of the chairs needed to be reupholstered, naturally. Where would all those chairs go? 'A thousand places,' said Charles. No such thing as too many chairs, apparently." –CASSIE SHIRES

"Charles once told me, 'If you are shopping and you love something, buy a pair if you can. A pair is more valuable—a pair of chairs, a pair of lamps, a pair of vases—even if you aren't planning on using them together, it is good to have them.'" –PATRICIA MASSEY

"One day Drew was discussing with Charles an antique officer's clock in our living room that is one of our favorite finds. Accessories depicting dogs being a favorite choice for Charles, he replied with a smile, 'The whippet clock in your master bath is the one I'd push you down for.'" –GINNY WEBB

"I was always amazed and inspired by Charles's talent *every time* I arrived to photograph. The beautiful rooms were photo-ready down to the smallest of details. Every pillow was, as Charles would say, 'poofed'; fresh flowers were in place; every book and design element was artistically placed and fires were roaring in the fireplaces." –JENIFER JORDAN

Above: The entire room in a charming Cape Cod bungalow is done in blues and whites, to showcase the distressed green of the pivotal antique Swedish secretary, creating an airy atmosphere. The coral-themed fabric provides interest on the blue-and-white ticking chairs.

Charles created a magical mix of rich red fabrics in the Jameses'
elegant living room, from the red velvet on the sofa to a pair of
French Louis XVI–style bergère chairs covered in "Rajah" by
Cowtan & Tout, far right.

"He would pull out all of these fabrics, layering patterns and texture, and I would just think, 'How in the world is he going to make this work?' Well, he made it work beautifully. He would always say 'Fabrics are magic.' He would start with his pivotal fabric and take off from there, layering with silks, velvets, stripes and chintz. It was amazing to watch him work." —MEGAN PHILLIPS, ASSISTANT

Charles pairs two Louis XIV–style giltwood tables to accommodate this spacious formal living space. Elegantly displayed on the tables is an outstanding collection of precious and rare antique tortoiseshell objects.

*Below: Porcelain brackets holding carved wooden urns on either
side of an antique French tapestry hang above a sofa covered in
"Soligny Chenille" by Brunschwig & Fils.*

Left: A classically styled commode from Aix-en-Provence pairs nicely with a gorgeous velvet pillow in "Sang Sacre" by Sabina Braxton.

Right: Neutral colors and a sisal rug are the perfect backdrop for showcasing the mix of traditional pieces and modern art in this spacious vaulted living room.

"Whether it is a flawless antique or a spectacular contemporary piece, a table is, after all, meant to hold things, Charles said. No matter how beautiful, a table looks lost with nothing on it. Charles would define a tablescape as an artistic composition of accessories on a table, providing the essential finishing detail."
–JENIFER JORDAN

Left: The homeowner's love of hot pink and green is showcased in her living room, from the painting by Donald Sultan hanging above the antique French limestone mantel to the mix of hot pink and green fabrics.

Right: The symmetrical placement of 18th- and 19th-century Chinese Canton porcelain plates in the "Famille Rose" pattern and sconces gracefully flank the Louis XVI–style stone mantel and trumeau.

Clubrooms & LIBRARIES

*B*ooks are like old friends: I feel comfortable surrounded by my favorites . . . Even when rooms seem to be overflowing with shelves of books, patterned walls, heirloom collectibles, comfortable overstuffed sofas and chairs, I gravitate to orderly, symmetrical arrangements with a focal point. That is really very much the way French homes look. By imposing order with balanced arrangements, one can insert beautiful objects and still not overpower a room." —Charles Faudree

"Comfort is essential to good design," said Charles. That's what inviting rooms are all about. But there's a misconception that elegant rooms can't be easy to live in."

In clubrooms and libraries, knowing homeowners would spend many hours there, Charles filled the shelves and rooms with their favorite things and favorite collections.

Ginny Webb shares, "One of Charles's strategies was to pick a few outstanding furniture items as focal points for each room. We were always looking for great pieces. At one of our appointments, after I raved about it for several minutes, I asked Charles if he had looked closely at the painted Italian commode next door. He responded with dry humor, 'Yes, I've rubbed all over it!' At the same appointment Charles showed us an armoire that while beautiful required some restoration. I asked if he would consider painting the armoire, to which he replied, 'If it will sit still long enough, I will paint it.' Both the commode and armoire became pivotal pieces for our playroom. Most of our appointments with Charles were an enjoyable combination of chatter, laughter, and design accomplishments. . . On our last appointment with Charles we furnished and selected all the fabrics (from his most recent line) for our playroom. He even had one last surprise—a tiny footstool covered in Louis Vuitton leather borrowed from a retired purse."

Modern art, blue-and-white china, a pair of antique iron sconces and a French settee covered in "Biron Strie Check/ Blue" from the Charles Faudree Collection for Stroheim paired together exquisitely illustrates Charles's talent in his and Bill's clubroom.

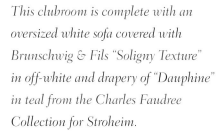

This clubroom is complete with an
oversized white sofa covered with
Brunschwig & Fils "Soligny Texture"
in off-white and drapery of "Dauphine"
in teal from the Charles Faudree
Collection for Stroheim.

Above: The Ratliffs' clubroom is in a lovely palette of blue, white and tan. The drapery is "Biron Strie Check/Aegean" from the Charles Faudree Collection for Stroheim.

*Left: Showcasing his fabrics from
the Charles Faudree Collection for
Stroheim, Charles mixes a palette of
raspberry and cream in the Webbs'
clubroom. The pivotal fabric is the
"Biron Strie Check/Raspberry" on the
French-style sofa.*

Right: A pair of Pindler & Pindler sofas covered in "Duane/Moss" corners the large clubroom in the Jameses' Cashiers home, with walls of impressive logs and chinking.

"There was nothing more charming about Charles than the love he had for his family, his beloved Cavalier King Charles Spaniels and his friends. I cannot recall a time when we worked together that he didn't mention his sister, Francie, his mother or a close friend." –KELLY GANNER

Charles chose the ikat in cream, mustard and burgundy from Kravet as the pivotal fabric to cover the four club chairs and pillows in The Casita at the Musselman ranch in Texas.

"I don't think we would have wanted to build a home without Charles's guidance and hands-on approach to every decision, big or small." —LAURA RATLIFF

"Nothing adds more to the warmth and personality of a room than objects and photographs of the ones you love." –CHARLES FAUDREE

"The guests were over-whelmed with our home's warmth and beauty and especially with Charles's ability to re-create the interior of a mid-eighteenth-century historic home with sublime colors, exquisite fabrics and furniture while making it so inviting and livable for the twenty-first century." –KATHY KUCHARSKI

"Charles told us he once used six or seven paisleys in the same room— we made it to four in our library." –GINNY WEBB

"I loved working with Charles because he always worked in my favorite things. He always worked in my sentimental items from my mother and grand-mother that I wanted around me in his design." –PATRICIA MASSEY

"Whatever the design and color motif, these charming spaces invite rest and relaxation, reading and reflection." –CHARLES FAUDREE

"While Charles justly earned an international reputation for his timeless designs and fabrics, we will remember his humility and wit every bit as much as we will his amazing talent. We will always cherish the fact that our home was Charles' final project. Charles left an indelible impression on our home, and in the process, on us." –LAURA RATLIFF

"He mentioned they were about to go on a trip to Paris and asked if we wanted to go. (As if there was any chance we would turn down the opportunity!) We went on that trip and it was every-thing we hoped it would be. An insider's view of Paris, the flea market, and the food and non-stop laughter." –ROSEMARY HARRIS AND TRACY SPEARS

Previous overleaf: This cozy landing features a delightful collection of bird's-nest prints. A bird pillow on a French daybed covered in green-and-white stripe makes this a favorite spot in the home.

Facing: A pair of Dennis & Leen wing chairs covered in "Pardah Print" by Lee Jofa flank a large farm desk centered between floor-to-ceiling bookshelves.

*Facing: This library also serves as a music room. A French daybed
covered in linen is piled with luxurious pillows for comfort.*

"Charles and his team worked for three days to move us in and 'voila!'— instant gratification. We loved everything he did. We wouldn't allow ourselves to place one single thing until he got there because he had that wonderful ability to place things in a way you would never have thought of.

"When Charles came for a 'move in,' he was at his best. Hanging pictures, climbing on cabinets to arrange articles, standing on ladders to adjust, and walking around with armloads of accessories. He loved the process of the final creation. To watch him transform a room was magical."

—LINDA JAMES

Above: One of Charles's home libraries with pecky cyprus paneling was the perfect backdrop for a collection of books and treasured canine antiques.

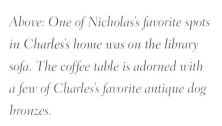

Above: One of Nicholas's favorite spots in Charles's home was on the library sofa. The coffee table is adorned with a few of Charles's favorite antique dog bronzes.

AFFAIR WITH A HOUSE

RALPH LAU

Facing: Alex, the Osborne family Westie, rests on the pair of Country French chairs upholstered in "Plougastel" by Brunschwig & Fils.

Dining
ROOMS

A dining room is more than a setting for bountiful dining and lively conversation. It is as much a room to display collections as it is a place for elegant and gracious dining . . . Welsh dressers, commodes, matching buffets and English breakfronts are perfect stages to display collections ranging from Imari plates or blue-and-white porcelain to Staffordshire figurines and antique tureens." —Charles Faudree

Mixing painted finishes and provincial styles of furnishings makes dining rooms more interesting, as does mixing upholstery and drapery fabrics. For added interest, Charles sometimes used different complementary fabrics on the backs with the pivotal fabric on the fronts of Country French chairs.

Wallscapes are another signature Faudree design element that have a significant impact in dining rooms. Symmetrical arrangements that include plates, mirrors, brackets, or paintings have a big impact. He said, "The things we choose to hang on our walls should have a special significance because they are details that set the tone of an entire room." Notes Kathy Kucharski, "His talent to hang anything and everything on the walls was without equal. (Even if it took several nail holes to get it perfect!)"

Patricia Massey relates that "once when Charles arrived, I was planning a dinner party. I had my plates on the table. When I came back into the room, he had all my plates on the wall! They are still there, I loved it and had to go buy new china . . . I loved working with Charles because he always worked in my favorite things—sentimental items from my mother and grandmother that I wanted around me."

Laura Ratliff recalls Charles feeling that none of her china patterns was right for a wallscape—until she suddenly remembered some beautiful Limoges that had been hand-painted by her great-aunt and passed to her from her grandmother. Charles thought it was the perfect shade of blue and immediately fell in love with it. The wall collage still makes Laura smile each time she looks at it.

The large, light-hued iron and wood chandelier suspends in perfect scale to the large dining room table in the Ratliffs' open-concept dining and living room space.

*Right: One of Charles's favorite buffalo check fabrics in mustard and cream covers
the dining chairs in Rosemary Harris and Tracy Spears' Cashiers dining room.*

"We favored antiques and Charles was happy to use them whenever possible. However, in some cases—such as our dining room chairs covered in a stunning Fortuny fabric and the unique corner cabinet in our foyer—Charles encouraged us to use high-quality new items that would be more functional and durable. He referred to these as 'tomorrow's antiques.'" –GINNY WEBB

The antique mirror with musical carving hangs elegantly in the Webbs' dining room. The drapery and the Piedmontese dining chair fabric is Fortuny "Demedici/Red & Silvery Gold."

Far right: Chairs upholstered in "Francois" from the Charles Faudree Collection for Vervain and an iron table with stone top bring a Country French feel to the Osborne's dining room.

Charles reused many existing pieces, just giving them a new paint finish—maybe a Swedish finish—and added contemporary artwork mixed with traditional pieces to update and create a new look.

Above: An extensive collection of antique majolica, with brackets and antique botanicals on both sides of a Belle Époque giltwood mirror forms a signature Faudree wall grouping.

"The true value of a painting or any other artwork has less to do with its pedigree than the emotional response it creates in us." –CHARLES FAUDREE

Facing: The Italian commode is a perfect perch for a pair of Italian altar candlesticks and an onyx lamp. Modern art hangs above in this beautiful wood-paneled dining room.

One homeowner says, "When he completely redid my dining room my husband walked in and said, 'I love it. Let's keep every–thing.' I immediately said, 'You have no idea how much that mirror cost, or these plates, etc.' He just said 'I don't care. Tell Charles I love it!'"

Far right: English blue-and-white china hangs symmetrically on each side of an antique Federal bull's-eye mirror with spread eagle cartouche in this dining room.

Facing: *The 19th-century Swedish pine table surrounded by 19th-century Directoire-style painted fruitwood chairs upholstered in "Menebres" from Pierre Frey were enjoyed by Charles's guests during many an elegant candlelit dinner. The chandelier was a favorite that moved to many of his homes. On the table is a German Metlock tureen.*

"For the ultimate in elegant lighting, nothing is lovelier than candlelight."

—CHARLES FAUDREE

The Jamaican dining room is spectacular with its wall of bookshelves holding a variety
of coral-themed treasures. The chair seats are covered in Cowtan & Tout "Tortola,"
while the backs are adorned with Beacon Hill "Fresco Stripe."

KITCHENS

"*A successful kitchen is one where host and guests feel perfectly coddled and comfortable. It is a space that functions both as a working kitchen and an informal living area; perfect for the kind of comfortable and casual entertaining people enjoy today.*"
—Charles Faudree

Charles often designed kitchens around the open shelving concept prevalent in French country farmhouses, and he used antiques and old wood to add history. He would add faux finishes to make new pieces old, such as on a vent hood or on new custom cabinets. He repurposed architectural salvage pieces for new uses, and used antique commodes and armoires for storage. Vintage armoire doors retrofitted as pantry doors was a Faudree signature.

Patricia Massey says, "I appreciated Charles's design because he always included function with beauty. He would even add a small table if needed to be able to set your tea or coffee cup down on while sitting."

Gayle Allen remembers she and Charles meeting a cabinetmaker in France to make her kitchen island. They explained exactly what they wanted, but the craftsman could not speak *any* English. Charles proceeded to explain in his limited French and strong Oklahoma accent, using a lot of hand gestures, until the Frenchman said, "*Je comprends*" (I understand). Gayle and Charles left with their fingers crossed, wondering what the island would look like. "How big? What kind of wood? It could be a gumbo tree!" Gayle says, "It was divine intervention; the island arrived and it was exactly as we had explained and it worked perfectly."

Gayle also remembers returning from that trip to France and buying a few French interior magazines. She showed Charles a photo and said she wanted the sink and bay window in her kitchen to look like the photograph. She said he was the best at making those shared magazine photographs a reality. "Charles really listened to what his clients wanted and his ego was never more important than listening to his clients."

A masterful mix of old and new in Charles and Bill's kitchen blends old architectural beams, open shelving and stainless steel countertops for a signature Charles kitchen design.

Rustic custom cabinets complement the original log wall of the James Cashiers kitchen, which is rich with antique treasures. Top middle: A Country French armoire front is cleverly retrofitted as the kitchen pantry.

Blue-and-white china is showcased in the Webbs' gourmet kitchen. Charles covered the antique bench in "Tanzania/Blue" from the Charles Faudree Collection for Vervain.

"We told Charles that we wanted a breakfast room table that was functional. We wanted the surface to be different from the wood we had in our previous home. Charles suggested a zinc surface, and he coordinated with his brother-in-law, Dale Gillman, to design the table. We loved the idea of having a round table that would comfortably seat six." —LAURA RATLIFF

The Ratliff kitchen showcases one of Charles's favorite buffalo check fabric, "Biron Strie Check/Aegean" from the Charles Faudree Collection for Stroheim. The breakfast table was custom made by Dale Gillman, Antique Warehouse in Tulsa.

Right: An outstanding majolica collection on and around a provincial wall shelf personalizes this breakfast room. Charles added a dough box beneath to complete the cozy French setting.

"Details are like frosting on the cake, and who doesn't like frosting best?"

–CHARLES FAUDREE

A fabulous antique window found in a Paris flea market was the beginning inspiration for the Shireses' kitchen design.

A Louis XV–style buffet that Charles had custom built in France becomes the center island. The top of a French cupboard was repurposed as a vent hood and painted to match the rest of the Allen kitchen.

"Each collection melded seamlessly with the ambience of its room." —KATHY KUCHARSKI

An impressive collection of blue-and-white china surrounds an antique architectural bracket.

"Our cottage was a very small project for him, maybe his smallest property ever, but he quickly understood that this was and is very special to us, and he embraced the challenge as if we were French royalty. What followed was the experience of a lifetime for me. I mean really! Traveling with such a fun-filled man to unknown areas, shopping from opening to closing, cruising the road watching for 'open' signs and stuffing the car with everything that moved us, from matches and light bulbs to armoires and portraits. Along the way he educated me. After I had gathered a substantial number of pewter pieces he asked how long I had been collecting pewter. I told him about 30 minutes! He said, 'Oh, no, dear. When you are asked, you should say, "All My Life" with a distinct southern accent.' Now, I have been asked and I do as suggested. He taught me about good 'whoop dee doos' and bad, how to hang oyster plates, the origins of a sailor's valentine, balancing and using pairs." –JULIE WELCH

"We were sitting in an 'off the beaten path' restaurant in Paris when a group was seated next to us. The woman shrieked when she saw him, scared us all to death, and said 'CHARLES FAUDREE! I have all your books!' Then she proceeded to introduce her entire family to him. He was always gracious about those kinds of meetings, as it thrilled him to be appreciated and recognized. He was truly interested in the people that supported him."

–ROSEMARY HARRIS

"Our first day of shopping, in the first shop I blew my budget! Charles said, 'Sissy, you better call home for more money!'"

–GAYLE ALLEN

"We were fortunate to go to France with Charles when we were building the house. Of course we attended the Paris flea market every day it was open. Many of the dealers knew him and would come out with greetings and embraces. He had an eye for all things beautiful and honestly saw things none of the rest of us did. He would say, 'Now, if you don't buy that, I'm going to.' So, of course, we did."

–LINDA JAMES

Above left: Charles's classic kitchen of red-and-white toile was featured on the cover of our first book. The 18th-century French Country drop-leaf fruitwood table paired with a 19th-century French corner banquette was the setting for many cups of coffee with Charles's family and friends.

Custom cabinets from distressed
reclaimed wood add interest in this
open-concept California kitchen.

BEDROOMS

*C*harles worked with me on at least eight projects over the years . . . He was a genius at disguise and deceit and was never afraid to throw in something from Pottery Barn, Wisteria, etc. Charles always told me to buy a ready-made bedspread, then he would customize the room with a custom bed skirt, headboard, lamp shades, and such. His custom lamp shades could break the bank but were always gorgeous," says one homeowner.

A master bedroom suite is often dressed with rich textures and patterns, neutral tones and room-darkening draperies. The setting is always restful and soothing, providing an oasis at the end of a hectic day. Enveloping yourself in warm, inviting comfort is essential in the design of a bedroom. As with the entryway, living room or dining room, the bedroom design process begins with an important piece or pivotal fabric. For a bedroom it is usually a fabric. "Color is the key to creating a bedroom space that will inspire relaxation. The color palette should be quiet, calming and restful, suggesting the feeling of a retreat away from the cares of the day," Charles said.

Draping the bed is a hallmark of Country French design, whether the drapery fabric is a gossamer sheer, yards of silk that puddle on the floor, an ambient storytelling toile, or any of the beautiful florals that give a bed a touch of forever springtime. When a room lent itself to that kind of sensuous, romantic draping, Charles enjoyed adorning the bed with beautiful fabrics and luxurious trims.

Using contrast to call attention to something is an artistic principle that has many uses in decorating any room, especially the bedroom. Also, layering pillows and bed covers made of different fabrics, colors and textures creates a cozy haven.

This antique French iron bed is gracefully draped with embroidered linen side panels. Charles created magic with a beautiful array of fabrics, colors and textures.

Overleaf: The Webbs' master suite has a regal presence for a night's slumber. The exquisite bed with the black and gold finish pairs nicely with the pivotal fabric, "Beauclaire/Teastain" from the Charles Faudree Collection for Vervain.

"Charles was an expert at mixing colors . . . to create a beautiful collage. He was fearless in choosing and mixing many shades of red or blue to great effect. Our master bedroom is a great representation of his skill and success, mixing peach tones with deep burgundies and shades of blues and greens."

—GINNY WEBB

Soft pastel greens, yellows and pinks form the palette for Brigitte Webb's room. Charles's passion for details is lavishly displayed, from the covered headboard in the pivotal fabric and white crown drapery edged in exquisite fringe to the custom window draperies and bed linens.

"What a character! Since we live in Oklahoma City we made many trips to Tulsa to sit in the fabric room, make plans, hear Charles's hilarious stories of meeting quirky ladies on his book tours all over the U.S., eating oatmeal-raisin cookies from Queenie's and just enjoying being in his presence. Appointments with Charles were always a very fun day for Elby and me. We laughed a lot!" –TINA BEAL

Below: The McCubbins' guest drapery is a beautiful buffalo check of "Chelsea Editions-Medium Check/New Gold."

Finishing touches in the Ratliffs'
master suite are impressive. The
blue-and-taupe drapery is "Glenville
Sheer/Slatestone" from the Charles
Faudree Collection for Stroheim, with
luxurious trim and Tremblay/Oasis
fringe from the same collection.

"When it comes to fabric, I'm from the 'more is better' school." —CHARLES FAUDREE

"Pillows are a wonderfully effective way to introduce more fabrics." —CHARLES FAUDREE

Charles mixed a modern bed with his signature Country French antiques. He designed a stylish custom dog chair to make it easy for Lila and Ruby to get into bed. The dog chair was fabricated by Dale Gillman, Antique Warehouse in Tulsa.

"Only your eye can tell you what you will be happy with." —CHARLES FAUDREE

Facing: Reds, creams and taupes make up the color palette of the Musselmans' ranch master suite. The duvet cover and European shams are "Braquenie-Le Grand Corail Toile/Multicolore."

"Charles taught us so much about loving, kind-

ness, generosity, acceptance and humor that it

would be hard to say what we appreciated and

loved the most about him." –LINDA JAMES

Above: The Jameses's master suite is tranquil with Charles's mix of luxurious spa-
colored linens and two beautiful trumeau mirrors flanking a lovely oil painting
centered over the bed. The European shams are "Imperial Plaid/Spa" for Robert Allen.

"He was the master at listening to and 'reading' his clients. With his reputation he could have been difficult to work with, but instead he patiently showed us sample after sample." –LINDA JAMES

"We now have the quilt he had on one of the beds in The Roost on our bed in our second home in Deer Valley, Utah . . . When Charles knew you loved something, he gave it to you." –TINA BEAL

"The blue and white chair and ottoman in the master were Charles' vision. He said he thought I needed a spot to relax, look at the golf course, read or watch television. It is my favorite place in the house to sit. Charles had a unique vision for each room, and how we would most enjoy living in it." –LAURA RATLIFF

"Whether you just met him or knew him for years, you felt as if he was your longtime friend. He could tell a story like no one else. From having dinner with Judy Garland, meeting five different presidents, or just telling you about his day, it was always entertaining."
–ROSEMARY HARRIS AND TRACY SPEARS

"The most important ingredient of a
home is that it must have soul." —CHARLES FAUDREE

*Previous overleaf: Beautiful hand-
painted twin headboards are the pivotal
pieces in the Jamaican guest room.*

*Right: Brown-and-white toile covers
the twin headboards and bedding in
the guest room. Surrounding the beds
are Napoleonic treasures.*

Left: Layered pillows and bed covers made of different fabrics, textures and colors create a cozy retreat in this master bedroom.

"If you fall in love
with something, that
is all that matters."

—CHARLES FALOREE

*Facing: Modern Lucite lamps mixed with custom paisley
lamp shades adorn George Fadaol's master suite.*

"Charles always called me his 'speed client.' When it was time for a new project, I would fly to Tulsa and he would have every hot pink and lime green fabric he could find with matching fringes laid out on the long table in his store. I would walk down the table and say, 'I love that fabric, let's use it in the master.' Then he would pull all the coordinating fabrics to accent the room. And then move to the next room; I would decorate an entire home in one hour, then I was ready for us to go to lunch. I just wanted to spend time with Charles and Bill, and hopefully Francie was in town. Then the installation would arrive and there were always surprises, like wonderful custom lamp shades. I would look at the finished project and say, 'I would have never thought of that.'"
—DRU HAMMER

Above: The Isons' master suite is a beautiful mix of pale blue, cream and mint.

Facing: Blue-and-white checks, stripes and toile give the master bedroom in Charles's cabin personality.

Facing: A grouping of framed botanicals, antique French mirror and a pair of gilded brackets holding celadon vases adds much interest in this cabin.

"He was a tireless worker, and we always felt like we had one hundred percent of his attention during our appointments, even when friends and former clients would drop by unexpectedly (which they often did)." —LAURA RATLIFF

Facing: A beautiful French table flanked by two comfortable armchairs sits in front of an antique English carved wooden fireplace in this wonderful master suite.

Above: A French painting from a Paris flea market hangs above a lovely iron bed in the inviting guest suite.

"I was completely smitten. Not only did
I love his design style, I loved him!"

—TINA BEAL

*Below: "Les Sylphides" by Marvic covers a French Louis XV chair and
ottoman that rest beside the cast-limestone mantel in the Ganners'
master suite.*

Facing: A wall of antique painted boiserie from a French chateau now adorns the walls in this cabin master suite.

Bathrooms, Closets & DRESSING ROOMS

"A bathroom is one of the most fundamental and functional rooms in any home. But it should be designed with elegance and lavished with as much style as the major living areas." —Charles Faudree

Kathy Kucharski says, "We were having a large luncheon at our home and Charles came quite early in the morning to make sure everything was picture-perfect. When a guest bath was shy of just the right hand towels, he did not hesitate to phone his dear friend and shopkeeper at home to request a special delivery of lovely linens to complete the look."

"The all-important vanity is the pivotal piece in bathroom design," said Charles. "And whenever possible, I will include a final finishing touch of a chair. The chair is, of course, of antique heritage and upholstered in fabric complementary to the walls and window treatments."

In one bathroom, Charles started with a pine fragment as a frame to a mirror and had a commode matched to transform an ordinary space into a room with warmth and a sense of history. Charles often repurposed antique commodes or antique desks as wonderful sink stands, or he would use a handsome desk as a vanity table in a dressing room. He also used antique armoire fronts to hide the utilitarian space of a bathtub.

Combining freestanding pieces with built-ins can add charm and efficiency to a closet. Also a custom closet with paneling is more elegant, with the paneling being used to create an extensive built-in closet wardrobe.

The mustard and gray Marvic "Les Oiseaux/Gold" wallpaper sets the tone of the McCubbins' guest bathroom. Charles retrofit a French armoire front to cleverly hide the bathtub.

"The details of decorating give a home its soul."

—CHARLES FAUDREE

Right: A lovely antique painted chest has been converted for a guest bath sink in Charles's home. Charles had a talent for reusing his and his clients' treasures in different applications in each of their next homes. The stunning antique mirror had different prominent places in his previous homes.

In Laura Ratliff's powder bath, Charles used one of his favorite wallpapers from the Charles Faudree collection for Stroheim, "Cashiers/Blue"; the squirrel and scroll pattern with oak leaves and acorns. Charles thought it made a wonderful backdrop; so did Laura. "Blue is the pivotal color throughout our home. We only used wallpaper in the powder bath, utility bath, mudroom and master bath. Each wallpaper was selected from several Charles suggested, but the powder bath was something we all agreed upon quickly. It was an easy choice." —LAURA RATLIFF

Facing: The Ratliffs' guest bath is wrapped in Charles's "Cashiers/Blue" wallpaper, blue being one of the owner's favorite colors for decorating.

Below: Charles enjoyed designing "his" and "hers" closets for Laura and Reeder Ratliff.

"So many people talk about the amazing experience of appointments in his magical fabric room. And of course even more fantastic was watching him zipping through the Marché aux Puces in Paris with his darling uniform of khaki pants, loafers and navy blazer—toting that leather-and-canvas bag. It was like watching Willy Wonka. He moved confidently through the furniture and smalls; his sense of wonder, excitement and pure joy when he found just the perfect piece was infectious! I learned so much just watching him work and truly had some of the best trips of my life!"

—MELISSA ISON

"Too much is never enough."

—CHARLES FAUDREE

Facing right: Charles converted an antique French painted buffet into a functional yet elegant vanity with sink in this master bathroom. A stunning trumeau mirror and a pair of antique sconces enhance the setting.

"I had the privilege of working with Charles on eight different properties. Once I began working with him I literally looked for homes to renovate and design just so I could be with Charles. I loved every minute of antique shopping, choosing all the fabrics and hunting for all the wonderful tchotchkes he would always find.

"Charles had found this perfect wallpaper for me, with green and leopard frogs standing up at attention. We had a few men come over from the Hammer Museum to help hang paintings for us. Charles proceeds into the powder bath with that wallpaper and tells the men, 'Please hang this painting at this crotch level,' as he is pointing to a line. I told Charles, Thanks to you, now all I see is a bunch of frogs' crotches every time I walk into that room. Every home since, I have used that wallpaper in each of my powder baths." –DRU HAMMER

Facing, bottom left: Dru Hammer's guest bath showcases another fabulous mix of her signature colors. The chinoiserie mirror elegantly hangs centered in her powder bath, paired with French bergère chairs.

Below: Charles had a passion for details. He combined antique French paneling with elaborate mirrors and cabinetry to customize this master suite bathroom.

"Accessories are as important to a room as the furniture itself."

—CHARLES FAUDREE

Facing above: Charles's closets were a testament to his meticulous organizational skills, displaying his signature bow ties and unique shoes.

"I walk into the last project we worked on together, in Dallas, and think of him every day I am there. He made my life so much better and not just in an aesthetic way. At night after working together all day, we would go to dinner and talk about how good God has been to us in our lives and even cry together at how blessed we are. All of Charles's clients thought they were his best friend; that's how he made you feel. But sorry, girls, I really was. Ha!" –DRU HAMMER

Facing right: A gold-framed collection of letter seals accents this closet. The dark wood paneling sets a distinguished masculine tone.

Outdoor
SPACES

*T*he decorating possibilities for outdoor living areas have been revolutionized by the improvements in outdoor fabrics," said Charles.

Any design is possible, for example a room setting is possible, complete with upholstered sofas, pillows, chairs and a painting disguising a television.

Screened porches were one of Charles favorites to design. From a lake cabin screened porch to a mountain retreat, he enjoyed using the comfort of indoor furnishings along with draperies made of revolutionized fabric.

French furnishings are often thought of as too formal, but the French have a countryside too, and furniture for rural entertaining used in outdoor living reflects Charles's love of all things French.

Below: This outdoor porch, with furnishings from McKinnon and Harris, has a majestic view of the Smoky Mountains.

"I will never forget the day Charles and April were coming to our home for an appointment. On the way over, he made one of his infamous prank phone calls. He called and, using his best old-lady voice, told me that the chickens in my yard were making too much noise! Of course, being the gullible person I am, I fell for it and informed 'her' that I did not own any chickens and that 'she' must have the wrong number. He had 'gotten me' and he loved it!"

–TINA BEAL

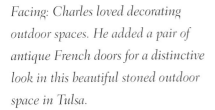

Facing: Charles loved decorating outdoor spaces. He added a pair of antique French doors for a distinctive look in this beautiful stoned outdoor space in Tulsa.

Facing: The magnificent view of the formal pool house reveals as much sophistication as the home's indoor rooms, including draperies and upholstered pieces.

"Charles's design impact was always the same . . . . [he created] true pleasure not only for us but for our family and friends, as well." KATHY KUCHARSKI

"While I was in my car I received a phone call from a distraught poodle groomer, aka Charles. In less than 15 minutes he just about had me convinced that I needed to go pick up this poor poodle I had apparently left behind. Getting more and more frazzled, trying to convince this woman I didn't even own a dog, Charles started laughing and I then realized I had been pranked." –KELLY GANNER

"My most treasured memory is the weekend I was sitting in a hotel bar in Laredo, Texas. I was on a birthday trip for a friend of my husband's and here comes a boisterous crowd led by none other than Charles himself! They were in town for a big wedding. That night when my group was across the border in Mexico on the way to a very popular bar, we saw a six-foot-tall piñata of an old-timey circus strong man. Knowing I had to play a trick on Charles, the ultimate trickster, my Houston friends and I bought it and carried it all over Mexico and back across the border late that night. While the Tulsa group was still at the rehearsal dinner, we talked our way into Charles's hotel room and hid the man in his shower, peeking out of the curtain. Needless to say, the shrieks and laughter continued late into the night and throughout the weekend as the strong man appeared in all sorts of mysterious places!"
–MELISSA ISON

Sunlight drifts through the wisteria to this California garden room, where a mix of floral, striped and solid fabrics create an outdoor oasis.

ACKNOWLEDGMENTS

I want to give my sincere heartfelt thanks to Charles Faudree for the twenty-seven years of friendship and laughter. I am grateful for the honor and joyous task of photographing his beautiful homes illustrating his incredible talent. I particularly want to thank my friend and Charles's partner, Bill Carpenter. Without his love for Charles, help and patience, this book would not have happened. And thanks to Charles and Bill's precious Cavalier Spaniels, Ruby and Lila.

I especially want to thank all the homeowners from the previous books and of Charles last projects who graciously let me photograph their beautiful homes and shared their experiences with Charles and the impact his design has had on their lives. They include Gayle and Steve Allen; Tina and Elby Beal; Kate and Stuart Beal; Bill Carpenter; the late Joanne Hearst Castro; Gayle and Frank Eby; George Fadaol; Kelly and Roger Ganner; Dru Hammer; Mickey and Tom Harris; Rosemary Harris and Tracy Spears; Melissa Ison; Linda and Darwin James; Kathy and Bob Kucharski; Rebecca and David McCubbin; Julie and Jimmy Musselman; Patricia and Clebber Massey; Julie and John Nickel; Bob and Ann Osborne; Laura and Reeder Ratliff; Cassie and Mark Shires; Ginny, Drew and Brigitte Webb; and Julie and James Welch.

Thank you to Hilary Rose for her beautiful photo styling for the James and Harris and Spears homes in Cashiers, North Carolina.

I especially want to thank my sister, Joanne Jordan, for always being there for me and for her help in writing the captions with her "plethora of expressive adjectives" when I was temporarily blocked. And thanks to my mother for her patience while I held up Thanksgiving Dinner to complete yet another chapter of captions.

Many thanks to Megan Phillips, Charles's assistant, for her stories and help in gathering contact information for the homeowners.

A big thanks to Darcie Blackerby for her help getting resources for the new homes that were photographed.

I want to also thank my dear friend Nancy Ingram, who introduced me to Charles so many years ago. Though she is no longer with us, I miss her and her friendship every day.

My thanks to Francie Faudree, Charles's sister, who shares, "When Jenifer first approached me about this book, I was a little ambivalent. For me, it was too early to let anyone in my life with Charles. But time has a beautiful way of giving one perspective. I know Charles would be proud and happy to see his latest work shared with all his clients and friends. I'm sure of it!"

Thanks to Madge Baird, editor, and Renee Bond, production editor, and all the staff at Gibbs Smith who helped in the process of putting the book together. And a special thank-you to Debbie Uribe for her countless hours spent gathering all the captions and images from the previous books.

And lastly, thanks to my precious rescue Cavalier Spaniels, Parker and Lily, for their unconditional love and patience over a few missed walks because I was so busy with the book.

And to all of you, Charles Faudree's readers, fans and fellow lovers of all things Country French, thank you so much.